Becoming Change

A Journal for Mind, Spirit, and Body

Francesca Russo

BALBOA.
PRESS

A DIVISION OF HAY HOUSE

Balboa Press books may be ordered through booksellers or by contacting:

Balboa Press
A Division of Hay House
1663 Liberty Drive
Bloomington, IN 47403
www.balboapress.com
1 (877) 407-4847

Print information available on the last page.

ISBN: 978-1-5043-4842-3 (sc)
ISBN: 978-1-5043-4844-7 (hc)
ISBN: 978-1-5043-4843-0 (e)

Library of Congress Control Number: 2016900817

Balboa Press rev. date: 03/02/2016

About Becoming Change

If you could change your life, what would you do differently? What is holding you back?

When you are happy inside, everyone you meet reaps the benefits of your joy. Sometimes change is brought upon us without choice, and as painful as change can appear to be, it is an opportunity to grow.

Becoming Change is a workbook to support and guide you through the process of transition and change. Read the book as often as you need, flip through it, and find the perfect page, or use it as a daily journal. When you come to the end, turn the book over and see how much you have changed!

Wishing you peace and comfort through your change.

Always believe in love.

Dedication

This book is dedicated to you, the reader, the writer, the creator of your daily wonderful journey through life. May you have the courage to explore its vastness.

On Being

You can be and do anything. Sit for a few moments every day and be that anything. Take some notes, make a few sketches, write a few lyrics, play some music.

Just be and enjoy.

Notes:

_____

_____

_____

_____

_____

_____

_____

Transition

The challenging part of transition is living life on the edge, daily. The great parts of transition are the opportunities that become available, opportunities that you never thought possible in your life.

It takes courage to trek into the unknown, even if your intention is to change your life in a positive way. Be steadfast, believe in yourself. What unknown or transition are you facing?

Notes:

_____

_____

_____

_____

_____

_____

Open Your Heart to Others

Change and transition open your heart to feelings you may have been keeping inside. Allowing yourself to feel, you become aware of others and their feelings.

Notes:

_____

_____

_____

_____

_____

_____

_____

_____

Your Body

Your body, mind and spirit are a wonderful vehicle. Working in sync together, they keep you healthy, happy and productive. Just like the computer in your car that tells you when you need an oil change, or you are out of gas, your body communicates when you need assistance. Aches, fevers, and discontent, are your body's messengers.

Has your body been talking to you? What do you think it is saying?

Notes:

_____

_____

_____

_____

_____

_____

Lost Keys

Do you have a pattern of misplacing your car keys, house keys or office keys?

Are you multi tasking every day? Take a moment, as you grasp the doorknob, and feel for all your keys. Ask yourself if you have everything you need. It is a great way to start change.

Notes:

_____

_____

_____

_____

_____

_____

_____

Playfulness

You are never too old to be playful. What have you enjoyed in the past that you have not done recently? Take time to play. Play with your dog, your children. Or have fun by yourself.

Notes:

_____

_____

_____

_____

_____

_____

_____

_____

Live With Wonder

Practice looking at your world with curiosity and wonder, as you did in the innocence of youth. Does anything from your childhood come to mind?

Notes:

_____

_____

_____

_____

_____

_____

_____

_____

Giving

One of the best things you can do for yourself is to help others. Is there anyone or any organization you can help by donating some of your time?

Notes:

The Dance of Fear

When you find yourself blaming others for the unfortunate circumstances of your life, you are dancing with fear. All things happen for a reason.

Take responsibility for your life; move beyond the negative of fear. Dance with trust. Your body will hold you.

Notes:

_____

_____

_____

_____

_____

_____

_____

The Ways Of Your Body

Take a moment; scan your body from head to toe. Is your head straight, and shoulders relaxed?

How does your lower back feel? Do you feel tight all over?

Gently roll your head from side to side.

Inhale your shoulders up back and down.

Lift your ribs out of your liver and stomach.

Take a few moments to relax your body.

Notes:

_____

_____

_____

_____

_____

Look and Listen

There is always something new and different every day. Sometimes the simplest little things will make you smile. Look and listen for them during your day.

Notes:

_____

_____

_____

_____

_____

_____

_____

_____

Fear of Trusting

Fight and flight is a survival mechanism built into your body. Trust is a necessary part of life. Once your trust has been violated, your body's nervous system protects you by telling you to retreat.

Intuition is also built into your psyche. Allow intuition to move you beyond fear at the right time. Write a note of trust to your fearful self.

Notes:

_____

_____

_____

_____

_____

_____

_____

Look Within Yourself

If you feel it is time to change, trust yourself. This is the first step into personal empowerment and self-love.

Take note of your innermost feelings and write yourself a note. Review this in a few weeks to see if your inner trust is working. What has this enabled you to accomplish?

Notes:

_____

_____

_____

_____

_____

_____

_____

Are You Afraid to Trust? 1

Take time to reflect on this question and list all the trust issues you have and why you have them.

Notes:

_____

_____

_____

_____

_____

_____

_____

_____

_____

You Have All You Need

All the answers you need are inside yourself. Listen to that tiny voice inside. The more you listen, the louder it will become.

Notes:

_____

_____

_____

_____

_____

_____

_____

_____

Self Trust 2

Before you can trust others, you must trust yourself. An example could be choosing relationships; perhaps you have rushed into relationships too quickly. What step can you take to slow down? What step can you take to begin trusting yourself?

Notes:

_____

_____

_____

_____

_____

_____

_____

_____

Push Or Pull

Are you trying to push or pull things into your life? If you are trying too hard, relax. Let them go, they are trying to tell you they don't belong.

Notes:

_____

_____

_____

_____

_____

_____

_____

_____

Intuition 1

Intuition is the voice you hear in your mind, or feel in your body that tells you not to do something, or to do something. Most of the time you ignore your intuition. Learning to listen to this voice or feeling helps you learn to trust yourself.

Can you remember times when you heard the voice?

Notes:

_____

_____

_____

_____

_____

_____

Create Your Sacred Space

Find a place at home, if you can at work, that will be your respite. A place you can spend quiet, heart felt moments with yourself.

Gather what is meaningful to you, it can be simple or elaborate. Taking as much time as you can every day, (even if it is a few minutes) will refuel your soul.

Notes:

_____

_____

_____

_____

_____

_____

_____

Practice Listening 2

Remember to listen for your intuition daily. Don't force yourself; let it come naturally. You will recognize it. Learn to listen and trust.

Notes:

_____

_____

_____

_____

_____

_____

_____

_____

How Do You Envision Your Life?

Know that things take time, and that you are in the moment of evolving. What would you like to see in your future?

Notes:

_____

_____

_____

_____

_____

_____

_____

_____

When You Ignore Your Body

As you move through life, ignoring warning signs from your body such as lower back pain, digestion issues, throat and neck discomfort, you are missing information that can help you heal on both the physical and emotional levels.

Pain is a message telling you something is not right in your life. Perhaps you need to change jobs or take better care of yourself. Make time to be quiet and open your mind. You know what you need; just listen.

Notes:

_____

_____

_____

_____

_____

_____

Releasing

Perhaps there is a person or situation you are ready to release. If you have a photo, memory or something symbolic, gather it. Using a sink, or a safe place outside, say some closing words and burn the memory. Send it back to the earth; now it is dust in the wind. Let it go!

How do you feel?

Notes:

_____

_____

_____

_____

_____

_____

Stretch Your Comfort Zone

Don't be afraid to smile at a stranger. Be compassionate and loving to everyone in your life, especially yourself. Is it a stretch? Or does it come naturally to you?

Notes:

_____

_____

_____

_____

_____

_____

_____

_____

Feeling Depleted

Healing requires energy. Allow your body some down time. Recognize when it is time to re-energize.

Notes:

_____

_____

_____

_____

_____

_____

_____

_____

_____

Self-Love

Self-love requires time alone to heal. Find time for yourself, even if it is a few minutes every day.

Notes:

_____

_____

_____

_____

_____

_____

_____

_____

_____

_____

Dispassion

Is there something from your life, you are ready to revisit with a new perspective? Forgiveness is both a powerful healer and an empowering, loving feeling.

Notes:

_____

_____

_____

_____

_____

_____

_____

_____

On Life

Life is a beautiful, sometimes challenging journey.

Notes:

_____

_____

_____

_____

_____

_____

_____

_____

_____

Fake It

Not feeling the way you want to feel? Fake it until you become it. What would you like to feel?

Notes:

_____

_____

_____

_____

_____

_____

_____

_____

_____

Those Repetitive Agitations

Pay attention to the repetitive moments of emotional agitation. A loved one, a coworker, or neighbor could trigger them. The agitation is a messenger for unfinished emotional business. What is the message telling you?

Notes:

_____

_____

_____

_____

_____

_____

_____

_____

_____

Remember To Breathe 1

Learn to identify when you are holding your breath. This usually means you are on overload and need to relax.

Take a moment and exhale, push your belly towards the front of your spine as you release air out of your mouth. Now you are ready to breathe in fresh air.

Notes:

_____

_____

_____

_____

_____

_____

_____

_____

How to Breathe 2

Whether you are standing, sitting or lying down, you can consciously choose to relax by practicing how to breathe.

Begin by pushing your belly toward the front of your lower spine, exhale the air out your mouth, and pause.

Slowly breathing in through both nostrils, allow your belly to fill with air, pause.

Exhale by pushing your belly toward your spine allowing the air to come out your mouth, pause again. This is not to be hurried. Go slow. Welcome to the present moment.

Notes:

_____

_____

_____

_____

_____

Utilizing Your Breath 3

When you have important decisions to make, act on them. Don't react to them. Take three slow deep breaths, bring to mind things you enjoy. Do this as often as you need to throughout the day.

Notes:

Breathe Space Around You

Once you feel relaxed from breathing, extend your breath outside your body. Imagine breathing a protective space around your entire body. How do you feel?

Notes:

_____

_____

_____

_____

_____

_____

_____

_____

Your Choices

Loving yourself begins the journey of transformation. Realize every choice you make gives you knowledge and the power to choose differently.

Notes:

Recreating Your Movement

Changing your receptivity to the world begins with movement. Is your body open to change? Pay attention to your body language. Are you upright or hunched over?

Notes:

_____

_____

_____

_____

_____

_____

_____

_____

Be Gentle

Always retain a gentle spirit with yourself.

Notes:

_____

_____

_____

_____

_____

_____

_____

_____

_____

High Five

Look in the mirror and High Five yourself, for everything you do in the world. Appreciate and acknowledge yourself. Make a list. Nothing is too small to ignore.

Notes:

_____

_____

_____

_____

_____

_____

_____

_____

Call In What You Desire, Push Away What You Don't

Take a moment to settle yourself in a comfortable space, bringing your hands in front of your face. Think about what you do not want in your life, and push your hands arms length away.

Keeping your arms outstretched, think about what you would like in your life. Bring your hands and arms into toward your body.

Project how you would like your day to be.

Notes:

_____

_____

_____

_____

_____

You Have Enough

You can always want for more, but the truth is you probably have everything you need. Take a moment to appreciate everything you have. If there is something you need to survive, don't panic. Write a plan to obtain it.

Notes:

_____

_____

_____

_____

_____

_____

_____

_____

Some Days

Some days are more challenging than others. On those days, take a lot of deep breaths and pay attention to your surroundings. There is always something to appreciate and distract you from yourself.

Notes:

_____

_____

_____

_____

_____

_____

_____

_____

Self Love

Loving yourself is not selfish; it is essential. Only then can you truly love others. How do you feel about this statement?

Notes:

_____

_____

_____

_____

_____

_____

_____

_____

Self-Motivation

What motivates you to get out of bed? Sometimes a cup of coffee or tea, a hot shower, or a bath are enough to help you start your day. Savor the moments.

Notes:

_____

_____

_____

_____

_____

_____

_____

_____

Rainbows

It is after the rain you enjoy the beauty of rainbows.

Notes:

_____

_____

_____

_____

_____

_____

_____

_____

_____

Look Up

Look up when you walk, look for the beauty around you.

Notes:

_____

_____

_____

_____

_____

_____

_____

_____

_____

Today

Focus on today.

Notes:

_____

_____

_____

_____

_____

_____

_____

_____

_____

Movement

Movement keeps your body, mind and spirit healthy. Do some form of movement every day. Some examples include walking, stretching, swimming, yoga, tai chi, or chi gong.

Notes:

_____

_____

_____

_____

_____

_____

_____

_____

Know Your Personality

Knowing what works best for you, what small step can you take today to be successful at your long-term goal?

Notes:

_____

_____

_____

_____

_____

_____

_____

_____

_____

_____

Self Love

What do you love about yourself?

Notes:

_____

_____

_____

_____

_____

_____

_____

_____

_____

_____

House Keeping

What needs to be done to lighten your load? Only you know what that means in your life. It could be literally cleaning your home, or changing relationships, or breaking old habits.

Notes:

_____

_____

_____

_____

_____

_____

_____

_____

Wherever You Go

Wherever you go, there you are. Stop running and distracting yourself.

Notes:

_____

_____

_____

_____

_____

_____

_____

_____

Bending With the Wind

Things don't always go as you would like them to. Rather than snapping, bend like a tree in the wind. You will feel better. You may even laugh at yourself.

Notes:

_____

_____

_____

_____

_____

_____

_____

Closet Therapy

Visiting your closet, rearranging clothes, getting rid of things, or rediscovering something you love, you had forgotten about, is great therapy.

Notes:

_____

_____

_____

_____

_____

_____

_____

_____

Allow Transformation

What is stopping you from being the person you want to be? Be honest with yourself.

Notes:

_____

_____

_____

_____

_____

_____

_____

_____

_____

New Life

Your new life begins by taking the first step, no matter how small. Write the small step you've taken or will take today.

Notes:

A Knowing

Sometimes you just know things. Don't try to over-think them.

Notes:

_____

_____

_____

_____

_____

_____

_____

_____

_____

First Step

What does your new life consist of? What has changed? How did it feel taking that first step?

Notes:

_____

_____

_____

_____

_____

_____

_____

_____

_____

62

Celebrate You

Pick a flower, or buy a flower, have a treat, celebrate you!

Notes:

_____

_____

_____

_____

_____

_____

_____

_____

_____

Compassion

Compassion begins within. When you find yourself behaving in a way you do not like, don't judge yourself. Observe and learn.

Notes:

_____

_____

_____

_____

_____

_____

_____

_____

Alone or Lonely

There is a difference between being alone and feeling lonely. Being alone can be empowering, productive, or relaxing and rejuvenating.

Notes:

_____

_____

_____

_____

_____

_____

_____

_____

Question Lethargy

What is the root cause of your lack of motivation?

Is it food or relationship related? Be truthful to yourself.

Notes:

_____

_____

_____

_____

_____

_____

_____

_____

Imagine

How would you like your day to be? How would you like to feel? Think as you prepare for your day, and that evening revisit your thoughts. What was similar?

Notes:

_____

_____

_____

_____

_____

_____

_____

_____

Be Courageous

It takes courage to alter your life, but you must be true to yourself. Unhappiness can become a comfortable routine.

Notes:

_____

_____

_____

_____

_____

_____

_____

_____

Notice

Choose to really pay attention to today.

Notes:

_____

_____

_____

_____

_____

_____

_____

_____

Change With Integrity

Creating change is not easy. When disconnecting from relationships, your intention should be communicating with compassion.

How can you speak or act that will have the least emotional effect on others? Ask for guidance. It will come.

Notes:

_____

_____

_____

_____

_____

_____

_____

Compassion's Roots

Compassion's roots are love. Pity's roots are ego. Every person's life experience is different. Having compassion for yourself and others means you understand this.

Notes:

_____

_____

_____

_____

_____

_____

_____

_____

Do for You

What simple healthy thing can you do for yourself today? It could be eating breakfast or lunch, instead of skipping it.

Notes:

_____

_____

_____

_____

_____

_____

_____

_____

Live How You Want the World to Be

You are part of the human race. Your individual thoughts and actions affect the collective whole. If you live in fear and anger, that is what you project. If you live with love and compassion, you will project love and compassion.

The choice is yours.

Notes:

_____

_____

_____

_____

_____

_____

_____

_____

Be Playful

Be playful today! Make jokes. Be silly. How does it feel?

Notes:

_____

_____

_____

_____

_____

_____

_____

_____

_____

Be Here Now

The more you live in the moment, the less you are distracted by anticipating moments to come, or revisiting moments that have passed.

"I think of all I am not, and all I wish to be, as I take my coat and go through the door. Outside, it is raining. I feel a rain drop land on the center of my head. It calls me back to this moment. The birds are singing, the trees are green, the plants are healthy. It is a peaceful, beautiful moment, and I am a part of it."

Notes:

_____

_____

_____

_____

_____

_____

Take that Extra Moment

There is always enough time to kiss and hug a loved one, and be kind to your animals.

Notes:

_____

_____

_____

_____

_____

_____

_____

_____

_____

Focus

There is always a positive in the negative. Find it, it is in there somewhere.

Notes:

_____

_____

_____

_____

_____

_____

_____

_____

_____

Quench Compulsive Desire

If you catch yourself craving another treat, running to the mall for another piece of clothing, calling another friend, scanning the paper for another movie to see ... STOP!

You have everything you need for life, and from life. Practice hearing the difference between need and compulsion.

Notes:

_____

_____

_____

_____

_____

_____

_____

Mirror, Mirror On the Wall

Mirror, Mirror on the Wall, teach me to love myself in spite of it all. Practice saying, "I love you" in the mirror. Try this first thing in the morning.

Notes:

_____

_____

_____

_____

_____

_____

_____

_____

_____

Who's in Charge Here?

Who's in charge here? Look to find the pattern in yourself that is controlling you instead of you controlling it. Stop and take notice; your body may be telling you something is wrong.

Take the time to go within and see what is not working in your life. Be patient. Loving yourself comes with practice.

Notes:

_____

_____

_____

_____

_____

_____

_____

Sharing

Share kindness, not grumpiness.

Notes:

_____

_____

_____

_____

_____

_____

_____

_____

_____

Personal Empowerment

Rely on yourself. You do have the power to change your life. You do have the power to keep a positive state of mind. You can have the discipline to eat right, to be drug free and alcohol free.

There are support systems, and many types of healthcare to support you once you have made a choice. The power of cause and effect begins with you.

Notes:

_____

_____

_____

_____

_____

_____

Envy

Things are never as they seem. Being envious of someone is only seeing what you choose to see. There is always a side you are not seeing.

Notes:

_____

_____

_____

_____

_____

_____

_____

_____

Calm, the Eye of Chaos

As chaos looms, threatening to consume you, remember: in the eye of every storm there is calm. Find your center, and find peace. Practicing calmness amid chaos in your life creates opportunity for positive change.

Notes:

_____

_____

_____

_____

_____

_____

_____

_____

Practice Being Calm

Sit somewhere peaceful, inside or outside. Quiet your mind by thinking of all the things that bring you joy.

Use your breath, exhale, inhale, and exhale slowly.

Notes:

_____

_____

_____

_____

_____

_____

_____

_____

Create Sacred Space

Create a place in your home to sit and be calm, or visit a place in nature that allows you to be quiet. Do this as often as you can. Use your breath to relax.

Notes:

_____

_____

_____

_____

_____

_____

_____

_____

Mindless Habit

When you begin to get anxious, what mindless habit do you have? Do you eat, or drink coffee, or wine? Is there anything you could do to change your habit?

Notes:

_____

_____

_____

_____

_____

_____

_____

_____

Your Inner Light

When life is getting you down, trust your inner light, surrender to the grace of God, the divine all-knowing, to illuminate your path. Clarity will come.

Notes:

_____

_____

_____

_____

_____

_____

_____

_____

Excuses

Relationships are supposed to be supportive, communicative, trusting, and loving. Don't make excuses for your relationship if it isn't. What can you do for yourself to feel loved?

Notes:

_____

_____

_____

_____

_____

_____

_____

_____

Live a Content Life

Practice breathing, and trust your heart. Things are changing, they always change, more so when they appear not to be. Practice breathing; trust your heart.

Notes:

_____

_____

_____

_____

_____

_____

_____

_____

Kindness

Love takes many forms. Kindness is one of them. You are being kind when you put judgment on pause, hold back a quick criticism, harsh word, rough gesture. Make your voice soft and gentle. Be kind to yourself and others.

Notes:

_____

_____

_____

_____

_____

_____

_____

_____

Self-Kindness

Refraining from self-judgment is self-love.

Notes:

_____

_____

_____

_____

_____

_____

_____

_____

_____

Again With the Mirror

You may be your own worst critic. Practice saying, "I love you just as you are," while looking in the mirror. The more you resist, the more you need this exercise in your life!

Notes:

_____

_____

_____

_____

_____

_____

_____

_____

Criticizing Others

Are you too quick to give advice, telling others the way you believe they should be living their lives? Practice lending your ear and listening instead.

Notes:

_____

_____

_____

_____

_____

_____

_____

_____

_____

Fear of Giving

Every cell in your body remembers painful experiences and creates resistance to giving of yourself. Honoring the past is important, but moving forward is imperative.

Take a risk and give from your heart; it will help you heal. How can you give yourself to others?

Notes:

_____

_____

_____

_____

_____

_____

_____

Natural Cycles

Allow your life to mirror nature. Like the seasons, what natural cycles can you create in your life?

Notes:

_____

_____

_____

_____

_____

_____

_____

_____

Beyond Judgment

Sizing people up is a form of fear. Observe people without judging them. Judgment closes the door to knowledge, and prevents new experiences.

Notes:

_____

_____

_____

_____

_____

_____

_____

_____

Move Forward With Your Life

NOW is the time to move through stagnant, unproductive cycles in your life. Take stock of even the smallest changes on your way to a better outlook.

Notes:

_____

_____

_____

_____

_____

_____

_____

_____

What You Eat Helps You Heal

When you eat food that nourishes your body, subtle shifts happen in your mind and spirit: you feel better, and your outlook on life is more positive.

Notes:

_____

_____

_____

_____

_____

_____

_____

_____

What You Say

Sometimes you say things without thinking. Forgive yourself and try to practice being mindful.

Notes:

_____

_____

_____

_____

_____

_____

_____

_____

_____

Take a Walk

If you have the choice of walking or riding, choose walking. Take a walk daily to exercise your body and refresh your mind. Don't let the weather be a deterrent. Dress for it: stay warm with a jacket, hat, scarf, gloves and boots.

Notes:

_____

_____

_____

_____

_____

_____

_____

_____

Signs

On your walk, look for signs that have positive meaning in your life. List what you found and what it means to you. It may be your favorite flower blooming, or your favorite bird singing in a tree.

Notes:

Words are a Signpost

If you talk about your unhappiness and desire to change, but haven't done anything about it, now is the time to listen to yourself, and make the changes you most fear. Words you share with others may point to the road you need to follow.

Notes:

_____

_____

_____

_____

_____

_____

_____

The Best Made Decisions

Taking time to be alone and quiet allows you to connect with your higher self. Ask for guidance, listen for your intuition, and trust the answers you are making the right choice.

Notes:

Values

Your wellbeing is much more valuable than "your stuff."
Think about what you don't need today to feel better.

Notes:

_____

_____

_____

_____

_____

_____

_____

_____

Be An Example

You can be a positive example for others, live what you love.

Notes:

_____

_____

_____

_____

_____

_____

_____

_____

Be Comfortable With Who You Are

When you live from your authentic self, you are comfortable in the world. Arrogance, boasting, and demeaning behavior with others are cloaks you no longer need to hide your true self.

Notes:

_____

_____

_____

_____

_____

_____

_____

_____

You Are Unique

Trust that you are a unique, special being, with much good to share with the world.

Notes:

_____

_____

_____

_____

_____

_____

_____

_____

_____

Believe in Your Greatness

Believe in yourself. Believe you have the power to change your life. When you live from your inner truth, you live in greatness. The wonders and miracles that will help you achieve your goals will begin to flow.

Notes:

_____

_____

_____

_____

_____

_____

_____

_____

Change Requires Letting Go

In the twenty-first century, letting go can be leaving relationships that are not working, changing a job that is causing you grief, saying goodbye to a self-image because you are filing for bankruptcy, or surrendering the home that has become more than you can afford.

Letting go does not mean losing dignity. Letting go with integrity allows you the strength, courage, and freedom to move forward. Free of baggage, you can begin your life again, lighter, with more clarity.

Notes:

_____

_____

_____

_____

_____

_____

Surround Yourself With Support

It is natural to experience fear and doubt when you make changes in your life, even positive changes. Surround yourself with people who support and encourage you. Your focus will shift to new possibilities and experiences, rather than dwelling upon mistakes. If you do not know anyone, trust they will appear at the right time.

Notes:

_____

_____

_____

_____

_____

_____

_____

_____

Beyond Media

Spend time every day without relying on your phone, tablet, Kindle or TV for distraction. Do this both at home and in public.

Notes:

_____

_____

_____

_____

_____

_____

_____

_____

Silence and Simplicity

Too often, without realizing it, you may complicate situations in your life. Your intention to help someone, or control a situation, complicates what could have been a simple solution. Practice silence.

Notes:

_____

_____

_____

_____

_____

_____

_____

_____

Effortlessness

Allow life to flow naturally instead of pushing. Removing force from situations allows everything to flow freely: serendipitous timing, the perfect parking spot, front row tickets to a show, the perfect connection to a bat, a golf ball, a volleyball, gliding over the pavement as you run. When you allow life to happen, amazing things show up!

Notes:

_____

_____

_____

_____

_____

_____

_____

Mind Blocks

Move beyond the mind chatter of self-doubt. You are worthy of love.

Notes:

_____

_____

_____

_____

_____

_____

_____

_____

Love is like standing on a precipice and jumping with free abandon, knowing you will soar. The heart has wings. Let it lift you into possibility.

Notes:

_____

_____

_____

_____

_____

_____

_____

_____

Embrace Fear

When fear comes calling, open the door wide. Embrace your fear and you will be blessed with new self-awareness. Name your fears.

Notes:

_____

_____

_____

_____

_____

_____

_____

_____

Smile!

Practice random acts of smiling at strangers, or when you're talking on the phone. Lift up the corners of your mouth in a serene smile. Your voice and your eyes will reflect kindness and encouragement.

Notes:

_____

_____

_____

_____

_____

_____

_____

_____

Time Alone

Do you need to take more time to be alone, or are you spending too much time alone? What small step can you do to change?

Notes:

_____

_____

_____

_____

_____

_____

_____

_____

Worry

The only thing worry accomplishes is an upset stomach, more wrinkles on your face, and sleepless nights. Why not allow life to unfold?

Notes:

_____

_____

_____

_____

_____

_____

_____

_____

Remember and Appreciate

Bad health, painful relationships and scarce finances cause emotional distress. Focus on all you have. Hardship and scarcity are opportunities for growth. Appreciate what you have and realize that things will change.

Notes:

_____

_____

_____

_____

_____

_____

_____

_____

Work In Progress

Be patient with yourself. Nothing is permanent; you grow as you learn! Think about the progress you've made so far.

Notes:

_____

_____

_____

_____

_____

_____

_____

_____

Stay Alert

Breathing improves your memory, keeps you relaxed, and stimulates your lymph system. Breathing keeps your body healthy. Practice conscious breathing daily.

Notes:

_____

_____

_____

_____

_____

_____

_____

_____

_____

Practice Breathing

Make time to breathe. Find a comfortable position in a chair, sitting on the floor, laying down or standing. Your spine should be as erect as your body allows.

Close your eyes. Exhale by pushing your belly toward your back; allow the air to come out your mouth, count how slowly it takes, and pause. Inhale slowly. Fill your lungs and belly, and then pause. Exhale as slowly as you inhaled. Rest a moment and repeat. Count as you inhale, pause. Count as you exhale, pause.

How do you feel?

Notes:

_____

_____

_____

_____

_____

Breathe and Detach

Sit somewhere quiet and breathe those long slow breaths. Become an observer, watching your life instead of feeling it. What suggestions would you give yourself to get through these difficult times?

Notes:

_____

_____

_____

_____

_____

_____

_____

_____

_____

Be Resourceful

Create a plan on how to move through this difficult time, do your best to follow it. Don't be afraid to reach out. Remember to breathe. Nothing is permanent. All things work out.

Notes:

_____

_____

_____

_____

_____

_____

_____

_____

Living in Transition

Transition is living between two lives – the old one that no longer fits, and the new one you haven't yet grown into. The art of living in transition requires acceptance of this.

Notes:

_____

_____

_____

_____

_____

_____

_____

_____

The Time In Between

Live your transition, (the time in between) with no regrets. Be willing to learn from past mistakes, as you consciously live with new hopes and ideas.

Notes:

The One You Are Waiting For

No one else knows and can love you more than yourself. Find a few moments every day to spend time with yourself.

Notes:

_____

_____

_____

_____

_____

_____

_____

_____

Do You Enjoy Eating?

Do you enjoy eating food? Do you enjoy cooking?

Notes:

_____

_____

_____

_____

_____

_____

_____

_____

When Do You Eat?

Do you eat when you are hungry? Do you eat when you are bored, sad, excited, angry, tired? Pay attention to your eating habits, notice how and what you eat.

Notes:

_____

_____

_____

_____

_____

_____

_____

_____

_____

The Effects of Food

Have you noticed you feel different after eating certain foods?

Notes:

_____

_____

_____

_____

_____

_____

_____

_____

_____

Stay With Change

People change all the time. The rewards of changing your life outweigh the difficulties. Staying with change takes courage. If you fall back into an old habit, start over where you left off. Don't beat yourself up; just get back on track. Spend time with people who support and encourage you. If you don't have any, it's time to make new friends.

Each day, live your new way of life. You will become mentally stronger. The benefits of positive change reveal themselves daily. Look for signs that confirm you are on the right track.

Notes:

_____

_____

_____

_____

_____

Be Kind

Today, be kind to yourself. What wonderful, positive kind thing can you do for yourself?

Notes:

_____

_____

_____

_____

_____

_____

_____

_____

New Beginnings ~ Old Ends

Change is the natural order of life. You are part of the natural order. Every new beginning comes from another end. If you are in a challenging place in your life, trust that you can meet the challenge. Change will come.

Notes:

_____

_____

_____

_____

_____

_____

_____

_____

Getting Sick

Change is a form of purging, releasing things from your life. Sometimes your body needs to cleanse as you change. If you get a cold or feel sick, be kind to yourself. It is your body getting rid of the old as well.

Notes:

Steadfastness

Starfish and sea anemone live attached to rocks with holdfasts that allow them to survive through drastic changes in their environment. Hold fast as your life ebbs and flows.

Notes:

_____

_____

_____

_____

_____

_____

_____

_____

Procrastination

Procrastination creates unnecessary pressure. Create a "to do" list. Notice how good you feel when you follow it.

Notes:

Your Inner Voice

Listen to yourself. You know the right thing to do. As new doors open, be prepared to be tested. Tests ask you how committed you are to the changes you have made. Trust your inner voice.

Notes:

_____

_____

_____

_____

_____

_____

_____

_____

The Slump After an Emotional High

After you have listened to your inner voice, and let go of a relationship, stressful job, or living situation, you will notice that your initial emotional high is followed by an emotional slump. Give it time. Live with your decision; try it on for size. Give yourself time to answer the question, "How committed am I to my life changes?"

Believe in yourself. Do not doubt yourself. Keep trusting. All will be revealed.

Notes:

_____

_____

_____

_____

_____

_____

_____

On Being Free

When you can rise above the things that bind you, in your life, you are truly free. Don't be afraid to let go of attachments.

Notes:

_____

_____

_____

_____

_____

_____

_____

_____

Out Of Control

When a relationship controls you, you feel powerless. How can you reclaim your power?

Notes:

_____

_____

_____

_____

_____

_____

_____

_____

_____

_____

Lies

When you live a life of truth, you assume others do also. It is better to trust someone until they prove themselves otherwise. Know when to move on and not make excuses for them

Notes:

_____

_____

_____

_____

_____

_____

_____

_____

Self-Reliance

The only person you can change is yourself.

Notes:

Unhealthy Patterns

Have you fallen into a pattern of allowing your partner to "get away with" unhealthy patterns that cause you constant grief?

Notes:

_____

_____

_____

_____

_____

_____

_____

_____

Take Time to Feel

Allow yourself to feel the wind caress your face. Listen while the wind plays a symphony as it rustles through the trees. Relax to the music of birds singing. Watch squirrels dancing through the trees. Take time to love life, love nature, and love yourself.

Notes:

_____

_____

_____

_____

_____

_____

_____

Control

Describe control. How important is control in your life?
How do you feel when you lose control?

Notes:

Surround Yourself

To live in the present, be in the present, surround yourself, with a clean, positive environment. Is there anything you can change at home or work?

Notes:

_____

_____

_____

_____

_____

_____

_____

_____

Tough Love

There are times when love requires letting go.

Notes:

_____

_____

_____

_____

_____

_____

_____

_____

_____

Your Greatest Ally is Fear

Fear can inhibit you, or help you grow. What fears have you overcome so far? Look over your list, or create one now.

Notes:

_____

_____

_____

_____

_____

_____

_____

_____

Good vs. Bad Fears

Intuitive fear protects you from physical harm. Projected fear comes from learned experiences, and it's often something you create in your mind. Practice knowing the difference.

Notes:

Live Life in Balance with Nature

You are part of nature, not separate from it. Connect with nature. Not sure how? Just sit and observe.

Notes:

_____

_____

_____

_____

_____

_____

_____

_____

Find A Tree

Find a tree you are drawn to, spend a few minutes as often as you can by it. How do you feel while you are by the tree?

Notes:

_____

_____

_____

_____

_____

_____

_____

_____

_____

Good Food Takes Time

Take time to prepare something special for yourself. Nutritious food will give you energy, especially during times of feeling unfocused, or lacking enthusiasm. You will lose yourself in the joy of the process.

Stay focused as you wash the food, cut the food, cook the food, and eat the delicious gift to yourself. If it doesn't come out the way you hoped, just laugh and try again.

Notes:

_____

_____

_____

_____

_____

_____

_____

Create a Feast

Prepare yourself dinner with unfamiliar food. Follow recipes if you need to but keep it healthy. Celebrate your life. Have fun.

Notes:

_____

_____

_____

_____

_____

_____

_____

_____

Live Dangerously!

Try cooking a new vegetable, perhaps something that you have not tasted since you were a child. You may be pleasantly surprised. You might like it!

Notes:

_____

_____

_____

_____

_____

_____

_____

_____

A Dinner Party

Once you have practiced cooking some healthy recipes, have a dinner party. Who will you invite? What will you cook?

Notes:

_____

_____

_____

_____

_____

_____

_____

_____

It's All About Me

Whether you are a giver or a taker, you are involved in a symbiotic relationship. Are you living and creating happiness?

Notes:

_____

_____

_____

_____

_____

_____

_____

_____

Unhealthy Patterns

Unhealthy patterns can be broken. Change the routine. Stay consistent.

Notes:

_____

_____

_____

_____

_____

_____

_____

_____

The Courageous Leap of Change

If you find yourself unable to sleep, unfocused during the day, lacking enthusiasm, or responding to others with a negative attitude, over eating, over drinking, under eating, over exercising, or if you feel like your body is wound tighter than you ever imagined, it could be your body is telling you to change.

Something is not right. Only you know what changes need to be made. Ask for support from friends, family, and your spiritual advisors.

Know that divine guidance will help you. Take the courageous leap into change, knowing there will be a safety net.

Notes:

_____

_____

_____

_____

_____

On Change

Any new beginning starts with the first step.

Notes:

_____

_____

_____

_____

_____

_____

_____

_____

_____

Living on The Edge

Put one foot in front of the other; look ahead, not below or behind. Living on the edge requires moment-to-moment focus.

Notes:

_____

_____

_____

_____

_____

_____

_____

_____

Visualize

Visualize your desires with clarity and complete knowingness, an intracellular vibration so powerful it recreates your destiny anew.

Notes:

_____

_____

_____

_____

_____

_____

_____

_____

Living and Trusting

Life will always be a mystery. You can live with the illusion you have control, even though you don't. Live life with trust. As long as you are actively following your path, know that you will be taken care of.

Notes:

_____

_____

_____

_____

_____

_____

_____

_____

Joy and Grace

Explore the attitude of joy and grace, knowing that you are evolving perfectly. Not sure what that means? Look it up in the dictionary.

Notes:

_____

_____

_____

_____

_____

_____

_____

_____

New Beginnings

Living in limbo feels endless. All things change. What new beginnings do you notice in this time of transition?

Notes:

_____

_____

_____

_____

_____

_____

_____

_____

_____

Pick Yourself Up

When you feel like you are being stepped on in life, pick yourself up, brush yourself off and start all over again.

Notes:

_____

_____

_____

_____

_____

_____

_____

_____

Non-Attachment

When you attach meaning to status and money, you create division, which then creates imbalance. Live from your heart, not your calling card.

Notes:

_____

_____

_____

_____

_____

_____

_____

_____

_____

Live Your Greatness

You are a miracle; you are unique. Every breath, movement and choice you make should not be taken for granted. You are an essential part of the greatness of all life. Allow yourself to live from the greatness that you are.

Notes:

_____

_____

_____

_____

_____

_____

_____

Think From Your Heart

Take time to be still. Listen to what you really feel, what you really love. Have the courage to act from your heart.

Notes:

_____

_____

_____

_____

_____

_____

_____

_____

Love is a Kaleidoscope

Love offers a kaleidoscope of color in your life. Find your colors and put them in your life.

Notes:

_____

_____

_____

_____

_____

_____

_____

_____

_____

Fear or Love ~ You Can Choose

You have the power to live your life each day with love and compassion or fear and anger.

Fear keeps your world small. Love opens you to endless possibilities.

Notes:

_____

_____

_____

_____

_____

_____

_____

_____

Loneliness

As you rebound from painful relationships, sometimes you hide your pain and move on without processing through it.

Don't rush into a new relationship because you are afraid to be alone. Reflect on the lessons you've learned, while taking the time you need to heal.

Notes:

_____

_____

_____

_____

_____

_____

_____

Laughing Therapy

Laughter is good for the soul and your face! It keeps the scowl lines away.

Notes:

_____

_____

_____

_____

_____

_____

_____

_____

_____

Take Comfort

Seek comfort in natural beauty.

Notes:

_____

_____

_____

_____

_____

_____

_____

_____

Find a Symbol of Support

When you go through your day, look for a sign of support. You will find it where you least expect it.

Notes:

_____

_____

_____

_____

_____

_____

_____

_____

Validation

As you are supported in your life, write down your experience. You can come back to the validations and re-read them in tough moments.

Notes:

_____

_____

_____

_____

_____

_____

_____

_____

Be Dispassionate With Your Life

The meaning of dispassionate: not influenced by strong emotion; able to be rational and impartial.

Training yourself to become dispassionate will allow you to make rational and impartial decisions in your life. When you are caught up in the emotion of your situation, you are not thinking clearly. Force yourself to do something else. Things will look different once you revisit the situation

Notes:

_____

_____

_____

_____

_____

_____

Flexibility

Trees bend in high winds. Grass springs upright after being flattened by a passing weight. You can choose to be flexible or rigid in your ways and beliefs.

Notes:

_____

_____

_____

_____

_____

_____

_____

_____

What's the Action?

What actions will you take toward your goals?

Notes:

Creativity

Living your own creativity is like watering your soul: it helps you grow. Everyone is creative in different ways. Find your creativity and live it.

Notes:

_____

_____

_____

_____

_____

_____

_____

_____

One Positive Step

When life is feeling stagnant, fear seems overwhelming; focus on one goal. You have the power to create positive change, one step at a time.

Notes:

_____

_____

_____

_____

_____

_____

_____

_____

_____

You Can Change!

Desire begins change. Action fuels desire. Together, desire and action change your life.

Notes:

_____

_____

_____

_____

_____

_____

_____

_____

_____

Achieve Self-Mastery

Self-mastery begins with the understanding that the power to change the exterior world lies in the interior of the self. Personal empowerment springs from self-mastery. Reclaim yourself. Share who you are with the world.

Notes:

_____

_____

_____

_____

_____

_____

_____

_____

Living a Nonviolent Life

Verbal violence is as wrong as physical violence. Practice speaking respectfully and compassionately with all people. Forgive those who have hurt you. You will open the door to joy.

Notes:

_____

_____

_____

_____

_____

_____

_____

_____

Look at Who You Are

You are your own harshest critic. Can you look at your reflection in a mirror without critiquing yourself? Learn to look and thank yourself for all the things you love about yourself. Can't think of anything? Thank yourself for being healthy, for taking you wherever you want to go.

Notes:

_____

_____

_____

_____

_____

_____

_____

_____

How Do You Love?

Allow yourself to be curious and open. Put aside expectations and judgment. Delight in the unexpected.

Notes:

_____

_____

_____

_____

_____

_____

_____

_____

_____

Meet Fear

Meeting your fears offers life-changing possibilities. Get to know your fears. You will discover that fear is not a roadblock on the road to your change.

Notes:

Trust Beyond Fear

Courage and action will guide you through your fear. Trust yourself.

Notes:

_____

_____

_____

_____

_____

_____

_____

_____

_____

The Eye of The Storm

When you are in crisis mode, find your center and be calm. Remember to breathe.

Notes:

_____

_____

_____

_____

_____

_____

_____

_____

Personal Empowerment

You are born with the power to direct the course of your life. Don't be afraid to use it!

Notes:

_____

_____

_____

_____

_____

_____

_____

_____

Study Your Fears

Put aside all distractions; give yourself ten minutes of quiet. Think about the fears that are holding you back in your life. Make a list.

Notes:

_____

_____

_____

_____

_____

_____

_____

_____

The Other Side of Your Fears

Fears are gifts of insight. Imagine what it would be like to have your worst fear come true. Then make a list of your fears and what you would do if you were not afraid.

Notes:

_____

_____

_____

_____

_____

_____

_____

_____

Respect

Respect is mindfulness of the mystery at the core of every life. How would you like to be respected by others?

Notes:

_____

_____

_____

_____

_____

_____

_____

_____

_____

Comfort

Taking a hot bath or shower can be soothing and relaxing, also symbolic of cleansing yourself of things that no longer serve you. Set an intention of something you would like to wash away.

Notes:

_____

_____

_____

_____

_____

_____

_____

_____

Test Drive

Test-drive the change you desire. Change the way you dress, put on something that does not feel like your usual self. Wear it all day and observe how you feel, how you respond to others, and how others respond to you.

Notes:

_____

_____

_____

_____

_____

_____

_____

_____

The Soul Knows its True Journey

The soul knows its true journey. Listen to how you feel. Allow yourself to live your truth. The world will follow your example.

Notes:

_____

_____

_____

_____

_____

_____

_____

_____

Follow Your Passion

Live what you are passionate about. Bring your life in sync with your passion. Begin with enjoying your favorite fruit.

Notes:

_____

_____

_____

_____

_____

_____

_____

_____

It Takes Courage to be Positive

When you feel as if you have every reason to be depressed and negative, be courageous and think positive. Act happy. Doors open with positive projection.

Notes:

_____

_____

_____

_____

_____

_____

_____

_____

Explore

Try a new route to work, a new coffee shop, a new restaurant to dine in.

Notes:

_____

_____

_____

_____

_____

_____

_____

_____

_____

Live Serenely

Throughout your day, notice how often you exert your will without compromising. Live life with respect for all, listen with your heart, and choose options other than your own.

Notes:

_____

_____

_____

_____

_____

_____

_____

_____

Harmony in Discord

Until you learn to hear, some kinds of music sound like noise because their harmony eludes you. In times when you feel most out of sync with the world, try to hear the deeper harmony to which you contribute.

Notes:

_____

_____

_____

_____

_____

_____

_____

_____

Anger

Where is the anger coming from? What pain is the anger masking? What are you not doing in your life that you need to be doing?

Notes:

_____

_____

_____

_____

_____

_____

_____

_____

Judgment

Heart blockages show up as judgment and cynicism. Recognize the signs, suspend judgment, dissolve the cynicism, and allow yourself to feel love.

Notes:

_____

_____

_____

_____

_____

_____

_____

_____

Beyond Resistance

If you are feeling negative, lethargic or fearful in your life, your spirit is asking you to change.

Be aware of your resistance. Find out what needs to change in your life. Once you have identified the fear, work with positive affirmations and positive actions in your life to shift your fear energy into growth energy.

Notes:

_____

_____

_____

_____

_____

_____

_____

Miracles

The first greens, pushing up through the snow, a beautiful, vibrant rainbow amid the rain.

Look for the magic and miracles life provides. What miracles have you been a part of?

Notes:

_____

_____

_____

_____

_____

_____

_____

_____

Signs of Fear

Signs of fear are: tightening of throat, loss of voice, discomfort in the stomach and chest, head throbbing, mind thoughts racing out of control, and the feeling of not being able to breathe.

What patterns does your body go through when you experience fear?

What patterns does your body go through when you experience fear?

Notes:

_____

_____

_____

_____

_____

_____

Release Fear

You can free yourself of your fear symptoms by recognizing them for what they are.

Face your fear, eye-to-eye, breathing deep, and take a risk. Feel the pleasure in moving through fear.

Notes:

_____

_____

_____

_____

_____

_____

_____

_____

Dreams

Dreams can help you bring closure with vivid scenes and people from your past. Reoccurring dreams can remind you of areas in your life you need to change. Pay attention to your dreams. Keep a journal by your bed.

Notes:

_____

_____

_____

_____

_____

_____

_____

_____

Feel

Practice opening your heart. Allow yourself to feel the beauty of the day. Share happiness with others. It is contagious.

Notes:

_____

_____

_____

_____

_____

_____

_____

_____

Release the Old

To make room for the new, you must release the old.

Notes:

Free Yourself

Write down everything you would like to let go of in your life. Check each one off, as you complete it. When you reach the bottom of the list, you will feel like a new person.

Notes:

_____

_____

_____

_____

_____

_____

_____

_____

_____

Mental Discipline

Minds wander, imagining things that just aren't so. Don't create stories. Wait for the facts. Practice mental discipline. Breathe, find something positive to think about, or distract yourself; read a book, watch a fun movie.

Notes:

_____

_____

_____

_____

_____

_____

_____

Confirmation

It is important to understand that your commitment to making change will be tested. Be strong. A sudden validation from the world will come, confirming you have made the right decision.

Notes:

_____

_____

_____

_____

_____

_____

_____

_____

Good Times

When life is good and you are on a roll, it's hard to imagine things changing. Challenges do come. You learn, you grow, and the good times come again.

Notes:

_____

_____

_____

_____

_____

_____

_____

_____

Curiosity

Be curious, ask questions.

Notes:

_____

_____

_____

_____

_____

_____

_____

_____

_____

If You Lived from Your Heart

Imagine if you lived in a world with respect, compassion and love. Living from your heart is all that is required.

Notes:

_____

_____

_____

_____

_____

_____

_____

_____

_____

How to Love

Listen to the needs of others and share, without agenda from your heart.

Notes:

_____

_____

_____

_____

_____

_____

_____

_____

Food Survey

Healthy food is your ally when it comes to positive living. Survey your cabinets and refrigerator. What living, healthy food do you have? What is unhealthy? Are you brave enough to throw it away and start over?

Notes:

_____

_____

_____

_____

_____

_____

_____

_____

_____

Fresh Air

Make time as often as you can in your life to breathe fresh, unpolluted, non-recycled air. Your body, mind, and spirit will thank you.

Notes:

_____

_____

_____

_____

_____

_____

_____

_____

Science Projects

Allot yourself ninety minutes to visit your refrigerator. Pull everything out, look for "science projects" in jars and leftovers, and check dates. Throw out all old food with free abandon! Now wash your refrigerator!

Notes:

_____

_____

_____

_____

_____

_____

_____

_____

Restock

Now that you have a clean, empty fridge, put food into it. Don't over stock, buy only what you will use and will be able to see. Try adding some new, healthy items!

Notes:

_____

_____

_____

_____

_____

_____

_____

_____

Change Foods

You have seen what you have kept in your refrigerator, you have a good idea of how you eat. What can you change in your diet?

Notes:

_____

_____

_____

_____

_____

_____

_____

_____

Allow

Allow yourself to feel love today. Enjoy the beauty of a garden, a hug from a friend, or a lick from a pet.

Notes:

_____

_____

_____

_____

_____

_____

_____

_____

_____

Transition Is Like a Shell

Transition is like a shell being tossed into the sea. As the waves crash on the shore, churning the shell in the sand, they are softening sharp edges and creating a beautiful shine. Transition takes time, be patient.

Notes:

_____

_____

_____

_____

_____

_____

_____

_____

Cycles of Life

Your life is an important part of the whole. There is much to learn from nature. There is a natural order to the changing of the ocean's tides, the cycles of the moon, and the seasons of growth for plants, trees, animals, and humans.

Take time to enjoy the natural beauty of life. Remember, you are a part of it.

Notes:

_____

_____

_____

_____

_____

_____

_____

Contentment

Being content within yourself changes the way you look at the world. Practice gratitude for all you have. You always have what you need.

Notes:

_____

_____

_____

_____

_____

_____

_____

_____

Change Is Like a Roller Coaster

Each day living in change is like a roller coaster: sometimes you're up, sometimes you're down, other times you're upside down. Hang on and enjoy the ride!

Notes:

_____

_____

_____

_____

_____

_____

_____

_____

Cocoons

Ever wonder what those caterpillars are feeling like, stuck in those small cocoons waiting for their wings? At least you can live and experience life while transforming!

Notes:

_____

_____

_____

_____

_____

_____

_____

_____

Light

After the darkness comes the light.

Notes:

_____

_____

_____

_____

_____

_____

_____

_____

_____

_____

Visualize

As you breathe in slowly, and deeply, visualize someone or something you love. Write or draw what you envision.

Notes:

_____

_____

_____

_____

_____

_____

_____

_____

_____

Expansion

Your life expands as you allow yourself to love.

Notes:

_____

_____

_____

_____

_____

_____

_____

_____

_____

How to Love

Listen to the needs of others and share from your heart.

Notes:

_____

_____

_____

_____

_____

_____

_____

_____

_____

Patterns of Fear

Listen to the number of times you say, "I am afraid."

Notes:

_____

_____

_____

_____

_____

_____

_____

_____

Live Out Loud

Live your truth out loud. What amazing qualities about yourself have you kept from the world? Live out loud.

Notes:

_____

_____

_____

_____

_____

_____

_____

_____

_____

Freedom From Fear

When you familiarize yourself with fear by doing things you are afraid of, fear becomes your teacher, your ally.

Notes:

_____

_____

_____

_____

_____

_____

_____

_____

Outside Interference

As you make changes in your life, your emotional and energy bodies are hypersensitive. Pay attention to how you feel, and how people you interact with are feeling. It is possible to feel other people's emotions. An example of this is enjoying your day, then suddenly feeling irritated.

Keep your mind in the moment that will help prevent this from happening.

Notes:

_____

_____

_____

_____

_____

_____

_____

Lifestyle

Courage is trying on a new lifestyle and seeing how it fits.

Notes:

_____

_____

_____

_____

_____

_____

_____

_____

_____

Sabotage

When you refuse to slow down, your body will find ways to make you stop, through injuries or illness.

Notes:

_____

_____

_____

_____

_____

_____

_____

_____

Dance With Your Fear

If there is something you have been afraid of doing, find the courage within you and do what you fear with integrity. This is not about bungee jumping; it is about living your life without using fear as an excuse.

Notes:

_____

_____

_____

_____

_____

_____

_____

_____

Effortless

List all that you do that is effortless. It may be doing laundry, cooking, cleaning, or gardening.

Notes:

_____

_____

_____

_____

_____

_____

_____

_____

Reduce Mind and Body Stress

Eating healthy food will lower your stress level and keep your immune system strong. How have you been eating?

Notes:

_____

_____

_____

_____

_____

_____

_____

_____

_____

Try To Whistle

Whistle your favorite tune. What did you notice?

Notes:

Our Teachers

Your greatest teachers are the people you interact with daily. Take the time to be present every moment. Who is teaching you something today? It could be the cashier at the grocery store.

Notes:

_____

_____

_____

_____

_____

_____

_____

_____

Live Your Truth

Live who you are, in spite of the expectations of others.

Notes:

_____

_____

_____

_____

_____

_____

_____

_____

_____

When Life is a Bowl of Pits

When it feels like life has given you a bowl of pits, plant them. Watch them grow and flourish.

Notes:

_____

_____

_____

_____

_____

_____

_____

_____

_____

_____

Acceptance

If you desire to be accepted for who you are, you must accept others for who they are.

Notes:

_____

_____

_____

_____

_____

_____

_____

_____

Assuming

Do not assume people know how you feel. Learn to communicate your feelings.

Notes:

_____

_____

_____

_____

_____

_____

_____

_____

Your Beautiful Mind

You have a beautiful, creative mind. Don't assume you know how a person feels. You may fabricate more. Ask questions.

Notes:

_____

_____

_____

_____

_____

_____

_____

_____

Awareness

Listen with your senses, what do you feel?

Notes:

_____

_____

_____

_____

_____

_____

_____

_____

_____

Listen to Your Talk

Listen to what you say and how you speak. Do you like what you hear? You can always change it.

Notes:

_____

_____

_____

_____

_____

_____

_____

_____

_____

Be a Respectful Listener

Listen to what people say to you; notice how their voice sounds. Can you ask questions instead of giving advice?

Notes:

_____

_____

_____

_____

_____

_____

_____

_____

_____

Respect Boundaries

Observe body language; if you are speaking and people are moving around, or looking the other way, they are not listening. Stop talking and move on with your day.

Notes:

_____

_____

_____

_____

_____

_____

_____

_____

Reciprocal Boundaries

If you find someone is talking, unaware of their surroundings, create positive boundaries. Acknowledge them, by making eye contact. Be positive and polite as you excuse yourself.

Notes:

_____

_____

_____

_____

_____

_____

_____

_____

Your Actions

Your actions speak louder than words.

Notes:

_____

_____

_____

_____

_____

_____

_____

_____

Separate From Others' Chaos

Do not allow other people's chaos to consume you. Know the difference between helping someone and allowing them to work through their own lessons.

Warning signs of the need to separate may include a stomach ache, headache, or loss of energy. Continue support with good thoughts and prayers.

Notes:

_____

_____

_____

_____

_____

_____

What Matters

During these times of emotional and monetary upheaval, remember what matters most is your health and your loved one's health. Count your blessings.

Notes:

_____

_____

_____

_____

_____

_____

_____

_____

_____

Cleaning House

As you face the need to change your life, tackle a house chore you've been avoiding. Clean out your closet, mop the floors, iron the laundry, or change the oil in the car to prepare your spirit for the work ahead.

Notes:

_____

_____

_____

_____

_____

_____

_____

_____

Forgiveness and Acceptance

Love accepts, love does not re-do. Love forgives without keeping score.

Notes:

_____

_____

_____

_____

_____

_____

_____

_____

Respond ~ Don't React

When you are in disagreement with someone, respond don't react. Practice breathing, it will help you hear what they are really saying.

Notes:

_____

_____

_____

_____

_____

_____

_____

_____

Headaches

If you have been challenged with headaches, it may be a sign of unrest. Is there something you have been avoiding in your life? If not now, can you correlate a past headache at a time of unrest in your life?

Notes:

_____

_____

_____

_____

_____

_____

_____

_____

Speak Your Truth

Don't let fear paralyze your life. Speak your truth. Open your mouth; the words will come.

Notes:

_____

_____

_____

_____

_____

_____

_____

_____

_____

Feeling Alive

Opening your heart, being kind to those you interact with through out your day (including yourself) allows you to experience that vibrant feeling of being alive. List your heart-opening actions.

Notes:

_____

_____

_____

_____

_____

_____

_____

A Song

Birds sing because they have a song. Find your song to sing in the world – whatever you do that brings you joy. Not sure, then it is time to explore.

Notes:

_____

_____

_____

_____

_____

_____

_____

_____

Loosen Your Grip

What have you held on to so tightly that you are choking it, them or yourself? Practice loosening your grip.

Notes:

_____

_____

_____

_____

_____

_____

_____

_____

_____

Adversity

Adversity is your best teacher. Welcome its lessons.

Notes:

_____

_____

_____

_____

_____

_____

_____

_____

Animal Teachers

Watch how animals breathe. They inhale slowly, and exhale deeply relaxing their body.

Practice breathing slowly, exhale, pause, inhale, pause, exhale pause.

Notes:

_____

_____

_____

_____

_____

_____

_____

Airing the Room

If you are feeling listless, wilted, and grumpy, open the window. Let the stale air out and bring the fresh air in. Stand by the window, throw back your shoulders, draw up your spine, and "drink in" the new air. You will perk right up and fuel your courage.

Notes:

_____

_____

_____

_____

_____

_____

_____

_____

Release Old Connections

If you find yourself over thinking a past relationship or situation that is making you sad, it is time to release stuck energy! Fill your tub with hot water; add a cup of sea salt and baking soda. Sit in the tub, say goodbye to the thoughts and let them go.

Don't have a tub? Create a salt scrub with granulated salt, baking soda, and olive oil. Rub it on your body and say goodbye to the old feelings. Take a nice hot shower.

Notes:

_____

_____

_____

_____

_____

_____

Love to Live

When you love your life, you love living. List the simple pleasures that bring you joy.

Notes:

_____

_____

_____

_____

_____

_____

_____

_____

_____

_____

_____

_____

Body Language 1

Look at your reflection in the mirror, both from the side and front.

Where are your shoulders? Is your chest wide and open, or closed and protected?

Pay attention to your hips. Are you leaning forward or are you standing upright?

How you stand, and walk lets everyone know how you feel without talking.

What are you seeing in the mirror? What are you telling the world about yourself?

Notes:

_____

_____

_____

_____

Cause and Effect

Practice self-awareness and gratitude. You will live and feel better. List all you are grateful for.

Notes:

_____

_____

_____

_____

_____

_____

_____

_____

Surrender

When fate dictates life to be a certain way, allow it; life may be presenting you with a jewel. Time will reveal all.

Notes:

_____

_____

_____

_____

_____

_____

_____

_____

_____

Have You Noticed?

Have you noticed your fears diminishing?

Notes:

_____

_____

_____

_____

_____

_____

_____

_____

_____

_____

Remember

Situations you experience in your life show your strengths.

Notes:

_____

_____

_____

_____

_____

_____

_____

_____

_____

_____

Learn About Passion

Learning about yourself and what you are passionate about in life can help you be successful. List your passions or explore new ones.

Notes:

_____

_____

_____

_____

_____

_____

_____

_____

Acceptance

Acceptance rather than blame for your circumstances gives you inner strength.

Notes:

_____

_____

_____

_____

_____

_____

_____

_____

_____

Those Days

There are those days when everything challenges your spirit. Don't forget to send out a reminder to God that you have "a situation going on down here!" Trust you are heard.

Notes:

_____

_____

_____

_____

_____

_____

_____

_____

No Victims

You are a victim if you choose to see your life challenges from that perspective. Life teaches through experiences. Is there a perspective you can revisit in your life?

Notes:

_____

_____

_____

_____

_____

_____

_____

_____

Choose How To Feel

"Easily I feel the emotions I choose, when I choose."

Repeat this affirmation, choose being focused, positive, content, loving or any other emotion for your highest good.

Notes:

_____

_____

_____

_____

_____

_____

_____

Edit Your Life Story

As you speak of your life story, and circumstances what are you conveying to others? Are you looking for pity? Or are you projecting the positive? You can rewrite your life any time. Why not start now?

Notes:

_____

_____

_____

_____

_____

_____

_____

_____

Celebrate You

You are a wonderful, beautiful person, so celebrate!

Notes:

_____

_____

_____

_____

_____

_____

_____

_____

_____

_____

Words To Overcome Your Fears

Expressions that stand for courage and action: "Take the drop!" "Let'er buck!" "Commit!" "Bring it on!" "Do it!" "Git 'er done!" What are your words?

Notes:

_____

_____

_____

_____

_____

_____

_____

_____

Peace

A sense of knowing and peace permeates your being; there is no tangible reason for this. Enjoy it.

Notes:

_____

_____

_____

_____

_____

_____

_____

_____

_____

Listen

Messages may come through a stranger or a circumstance. Notice how your body reacts. That is your intuition. Write down experiences that come to mind.

Notes:

_____

_____

_____

_____

_____

_____

_____

_____

Light at the End of the Tunnel

There is light at the end of a long, dark tunnel; this time of transition is soon to become change.

Notes:

Get Up And Boogie

Let loose ... put on your favorite music and dance!

Notes:

Your Life Makes a Difference

Your actions affect other people's lives every day. Take the time to be kind to strangers. Pick up trash instead of stepping over it. Let someone into your lane during rush hour. Help make someone's day happy.

Live your life from your heart you are a living example for the world.

Notes:

_____

_____

_____

_____

_____

_____

_____

Trust

Life can feel like you are standing in the middle of a seesaw, one foot on the low side, the other on the high side; the balance between having everything and nothing.

Trust, all things work out.

Notes:

_____

_____

_____

_____

_____

_____

_____

_____

Feeling Supported

You are always supported. This simple exercise will remind you. Lean against a wall, your spine from your neck to your hips should be on the wall, arms relaxed at your sides.

Your feet will be 10 to 12 inches away from the wall. Relax your legs. Beginning with your head, slowly allow your head to bend forward. Naturally your neck, shoulders and arms will follow. As your body leans forward and down, your hips will rise. Your body will stop naturally if you allow it. Your fingers may touch the floor. Slowly inhale, then slowly exhale. As you inhale, again lean into the wall, and slowly come up. As your body rises up the wall, your hips will slide down the wall.

Take a few inhalations and exhalations. Do this often, it is relaxing and supporting.

Notes:

_____

_____

_____

Silence

There is a gift in silence. It allows you to be with yourself.

Notes:

_____

_____

_____

_____

_____

_____

_____

_____

_____

Like Gravity

A wonderful, loving support system surrounds you. It is like gravity, invisible, and always present. Allow yourself to feel loved and supported.

Notes:

_____

_____

_____

_____

_____

_____

_____

_____

Wherever You Go

Wherever you go, there you are! Listen to yourself; what do you need? Is it to feel loved and supported?

Notes:

_____

_____

_____

_____

_____

_____

_____

_____

_____

_____

Validation

Yes, you need to be validated for the person you are, the challenges in your life. Honor who you are! You know better than anyone how far you have come in your life.

Notes:

_____

_____

_____

_____

_____

_____

_____

_____

_____

Expectations

What do you expect from others? What do you expect from yourself?

Notes:

_____

_____

_____

_____

_____

_____

_____

_____

Don't Be Shy

Kind words and actions are always appreciated. Don't be shy! Be kind to someone you don't know. It may make both your days.

Notes:

_____

_____

_____

_____

_____

_____

_____

_____

Twirling

If you feel like twirling, twirl! Have fun; you may start a new fad.

Notes:

_____

_____

_____

_____

_____

_____

_____

_____

_____

A Date With Yourself

Plan some time, to do what you love. No phones, no company, no distractions. It may be journaling, watching your favorite movie, having a delicious dinner or reading in the tub. What will you do?

Notes:

_____

_____

_____

_____

_____

_____

_____

_____

There is Always More

There is always more than meets the eye, in any given situation. Be patient, don't assume.

Notes:

_____

_____

_____

_____

_____

_____

_____

_____

_____

Fake It

Statistics have proven if you fake it, you will create it. What do you want to create in your life?

Notes:

_____

_____

_____

_____

_____

_____

_____

_____

_____

Value

Is there someone or something in your life that you care about, but you are allowing your ego to get in the way?

Notes:

_____

_____

_____

_____

_____

_____

_____

_____

_____

_____

Restore and Relax

This can be modified for anyone! Kids from two years old to eighty enjoy this relaxing pose. It lengthens the spine, reduces inflammation in the feet, swelling in the legs; it lengthens the arms and calms the mind.

Grab a bed pillow, sit on the floor, and slowly put your legs up the wall. (If you have sciatica keep your legs at a 45-, not a 90-degree angle) Lay back flat on the floor, legs up the wall. Place a pillow above your head to support your arms as you extend them up back and behind you. If you were looking at yourself, you would look like the letter L. If you need support under your neck, roll up a washcloth and put it under your neck. Lay here while you inhale through your nose, and exhale out your mouth. Breathe three full breaths. How do you feel?

Notes:

_____

_____

_____

_____

How Do You Relax?

What relaxes you? How often do you allow yourself to relax? What can you do for a few minutes every day to relax?

Notes:

_____

_____

_____

_____

_____

_____

_____

_____

When You Get Too Anxious

Feeling overwhelmed, ignored, the sense your life is out of control can create shortness of breath, and discomfort in your chest. This can trigger fear, causing more lack of oxygen. If you are by a wall, do the wall hang; this allows you to feel supported. With your head low, blood and oxygen go to your brain, helping you to relax and think clearer.

If you are standing, bend at the waist, allow your head to dangle at your knees. If you are sitting, put your head between your knees. Breathe slowly through your nose, exhale out your mouth. Try to listen to the noises around you, the smells, coming into your nose.

Come back to your breath, and breathe.

Notes:

_____

_____

_____

_____

Music Heals

Play music you know will soothe you, or make you dance and sing! You know what you need to feel good. If you play an instrument, play!

Notes:

_____

_____

_____

_____

_____

_____

_____

_____

Drama

How would you describe your life? Is drama a part of your life? Do you enjoy it?

What part do you play in the drama?

Notes:

_____

_____

_____

_____

_____

_____

_____

_____

Dehydration

A pattern of not drinking enough water, combined with caffeine and sugar, dehydrates your skin, your cells, your brain, raises your blood pressure, can cause dizziness and will assist you in making bad decisions in your life because your mind is not thinking clearly.

You should be drinking half your weight in ounces of water. If you weigh 150 pounds, drink 75 ounces of water a day, or do your best.

Add some mint, orange, lemon, lime, or cucumber to your water. Be creative, drink up!

Notes:

_____

_____

_____

_____

_____

Project Positive

Your body language communicates with people before you speak. Standing tall, shoulders back, head forward, projects a positive, open person. You breathe deeper, moving more oxygen through your body allows you to think clearer you are more present to your surroundings.

Pay attention to your posture!

Notes:

_____

_____

_____

_____

_____

_____

_____

Being Grounded

A grounded person is clear minded, present to their surroundings, makes realistic choices in their life. They look strong and focused. They walk connected to the earth. If you are over thinking, not paying attention, taking time to ground would be most beneficial for you.

What do you notice about yourself? Follow the grounding exercises on the next few pages.

Notes:

_____

_____

_____

_____

_____

_____

Standing Straight

Stand, close your eyes, and pay attention to your body. Do you feel like you are standing up straight? If the answer is no, keeping your eyes closed, find out where you are crooked. Are you leaning forward? Does one shoulder feel higher than the other? Does one leg feel longer than the other?

Try to stand erect. Feel the bottoms of your feet, inhale your shoulders up back and down, lift your ribs up and out of your liver. Now how do you feel?

Notes:

_____

_____

_____

_____

_____

_____

Practice The Walk

Walk around your home standing erect. Feeling the placement of each foot. Spine elongated, shoulders open and back. It may feel awkward at first. It will become more comfortable.

What do you notice about your posture? Is this easy?

Notes:

_____

_____

_____

_____

_____

_____

_____

A New Way of Walking

Take your erect, open posture out into the world. Walking tall, your head erect, shoulders back how do you feel? Besides feeling a little stiff, look around, are people noticing you? How does that feel?

Notes:

Eye Contact I

Acknowledge the people around you as you walk tall and erect, make eye contact if appropriate.

Notes:

_____

_____

_____

_____

_____

_____

_____

_____

_____

Eye Contact II

Respect the people you interact with daily, make eye contact.

Notes:

_____

_____

_____

_____

_____

_____

_____

_____

_____

When You Change the Way You See the World

As you practice walking erect, being conscious of the world around you, what do you see? Do things feel different? Do things look different? When you change the way you see things, the way you see the world changes.

Notes:

_____

_____

_____

_____

_____

_____

_____

Road Map

Have you created a road map for your life that allows you to connect to endless possibilities?

Notes:

_____

_____

_____

_____

_____

_____

_____

_____

_____

Detours Are New Adventures

When blocks appear in your life, follow the detour! It is time for a new adventure! Take a deep breath and enjoy the ride.

Notes:

_____

_____

_____

_____

_____

_____

_____

_____

How Do You Wear Your Shoes?

The soles of your shoes should wear evenly. Look at your favorite shoes. How are you wearing them down? Does it correlate with aches or feelings of being off balance?

Notes:

_____

_____

_____

_____

_____

_____

_____

_____

Grounding Homework

Stand straight, feet hip-width apart. Lift your ribs up and out of your liver, your shoulders up back and down. Lengthen your neck, so your chin is parallel to the floor, your eyes open, gazing forward.

Notice: Do you lean on the inside of your arches, or do you lean on the outside of your feet?

How can you correct your feet so you stand with your weight distributed evenly and continue to stand erect?

Notes:

_____

_____

_____

_____

_____

_____

The Grounding Stance

Remember to stand in your grounding position every day. You can stand grounded as you wait on line, in the morning before you begin your day.

How have you brought the grounding stance into your daily life?

Notes:

_____

_____

_____

_____

_____

_____

_____

_____

Grounding And Breathing

As you stand, connected to your feet, feeling tall and balanced, use your breath. Inhale; imagine yourself connecting the soles of your feet into your favorite soil. Maybe it is the warm sand. Exhale slowly. Try to feel and breathe your feet into the earth for three to five breaths.

How do you feel?

Notes:

_____

_____

_____

_____

_____

_____

Your Mountain Pose

Do you have a favorite mountain? Visualize your mountain. Stand in your grounding stance. Let your feet be the base of the mountain, your head its peak. Use your breath, inhale slowly, and exhale slow and deep. Feel the power and presence of your mountain.

Notes:

_____

_____

_____

_____

_____

_____

_____

_____

Power In Presence

Mountains are silent; they inspire us with their grandeur and presence. How can you bring that into your life?

Notes:

_____

_____

_____

_____

_____

_____

_____

_____

_____

Power In Listening

Imagine what your mountain hears in a day, in each season. Are the sounds different at the peak compared to its base?

Write it down.

Notes:

_____

_____

_____

_____

_____

_____

_____

_____

Becoming Your Tree

Think about your favorite tree, what do you particularly love about it? Is it the branches, trunk, leaves, blossoms, or the way the roots grow?

Write about your tree? How does your tree resemble you?

Notes:

_____

_____

_____

_____

_____

_____

_____

_____

Your Tree Pose

Stand in your grounding stance, feeling the soles of your feet connected to the floor. Move your weight onto your right foot, then your left. Which foot feels ready to support all your weight at this moment?

Once you have chosen your weight bearing foot, slowly bring the heel of the other foot up your standing foot's inner leg. Only go as high as you can stay balanced. (Some may make it to the ankle, others to their inner thigh.) Bring your hands together in prayer in front of your body, chest height.

Think of your tree as you inhale, slowly exhale. If balanced, bring your arms above your head, like the branches of your tree. Breathe deeply and slowly. How do you feel?

Notes:

_____

_____

_____

_____

Soles and Soul's Connection

The soles of your feet are your soul's connection to the earth. How do you feel about this statement?

Notes:

_____

_____

_____

_____

_____

_____

_____

_____

_____

_____

Going Deeper

The more comfortable you become with balancing in your tree pose, let your feet become roots, going deeper in to the earth. Use your breath to stay balanced, keeping your spine long, your arms extended above as your branches. Do this with both feet. This posture will keep you grounded, alert and balanced.

Notes:

_____

_____

_____

_____

_____

_____

_____

_____

Your Favorite Flower

What is your favorite flower? Do you have more than one? What do you enjoy most about them? The smell, color or shape?

Notes:

_____

_____

_____

_____

_____

_____

_____

Create a Bouquet Map

If you were to make a bouquet, where would each flower go? How long have you loved each flower and why? Paint or write about your bouquet.

Notes:

_____

_____

_____

_____

_____

_____

_____

_____

The Destination

Have you noticed, your destination becomes a resting stop? As does the next one and the next. Find pleasure in every moment.

Notes:

_____

_____

_____

_____

_____

_____

_____

_____

The Illusion of Perfection

Everything is always perfect. It is just not your idea of perfection, at this moment in time.

Notes:

_____

_____

_____

_____

_____

_____

_____

_____

_____

Self Survey

Is there something new you have learned about yourself?

Notes:

_____

_____

_____

_____

_____

_____

_____

_____

_____

An Understanding

Can you feel your inner recognition of oneness with all life?

Notes:

_____

_____

_____

_____

_____

_____

_____

_____

_____

Your Heart is a Bridge

Expanding your heart creates a bridge, connecting others to love.

Notes:

_____

_____

_____

_____

_____

_____

_____

_____

_____

_____

Heart and Body Opening

Lay on the floor. Your knees are bent, hip width apart, heels close to the back of your thighs, knees above your ankles. Your arms are at your side, neck relaxed.

Inhale slowly as you lift your hips up toward the ceiling. Pay attention to your neck and low back. (If there is any discomfort, slowly come towards the floor, finding a pain free zone.)

Your hips and belly may be high enough that you will not see your knees; stay in this position. Inhale through your nose, exhale out of your mouth, and try to keep your body here for at least three full breaths.

On the last exhale, beginning at your neck, bring your spine back to the floor, one disk at a time. When your lower spine is on the floor, lift your hips up once more. Do three cycles. Once complete, lengthen your legs, lay quiet.

Notes:

_____

_____

Wealth Is A State Of Mind

You are as rich or poor as you choose to feel. Being alive, with a sound mind, able to do everything you need is wealth. Think of everything you have, feel your wealth.

Notes:

_____

_____

_____

_____

_____

_____

_____

_____

The Morning Sun

There is a reason humans since the beginning of time situate their dwellings to receive the morning sun. The sun replenishes.

Take some time, sit quietly in the morning sun, (even through a window) breathe slow and deep, smile, allow the morning sun to nourish and replenish you.

Notes:

_____

_____

_____

_____

_____

_____

_____

Sudden Flashes

As you begin to release the barriers around your heart, you may have a flash of a past emotion or memory.

Acknowledge the flash as it leaves. You have just made room for more love.

Notes:

_____

_____

_____

_____

_____

_____

_____

_____

Tears Of Joy

Your heart expands, as you allow it. You may notice a sensation in your chest, followed by tears. Heart openings are accompanied by tears of joy. It means your heart is opening and growing! Congratulations!

Notes:

_____

_____

_____

_____

_____

_____

_____

_____

The Heart Knows

The heart knows what the brain does not. The sensations that you feel in your heart are interpreted by your brain the best it can. The heart does not need to interpret, it just knows.

Notes:

_____

_____

_____

_____

_____

_____

_____

_____

Every Moment Is Perfect

Life seems softer and easier when you take life moment by moment.

Notes:

_____

_____

_____

_____

_____

_____

_____

_____

_____

Riding the Waves

Waves roll, rise, crest then break, each one carves out the ocean floor below. Their work is revealed at low tide.

Your life rolls, rises, crests, then breaks, carving the floor of your life. Your work will be revealed at the perfect time. Trust the process.

Notes:

Receiving Pose

Sit or stand, with both of your feet consciously connected to the floor. Lift your ribs up out of your liver. Inhale as you open your arms out even with your shoulders, palms face forward.

Allow yourself to experience the sensation of being open to receive. Breathe slowly and deeply for at least three full breaths. How do you feel?

Notes:

_____

_____

_____

_____

_____

_____

Your Energy

There are many levels of energy that create the universe. Your energy is an integral part of the composition that creates this world.

Notes:

_____

_____

_____

_____

_____

_____

_____

_____

Attracting Positive Energy

Sit erect, hands on thighs, palms up. Feet are consciously placed on the floor. Set an intention, to receive beautiful loving, light energy. Use your breath to exhale out your mouth, pushing your belly into the front of your spine. Inhale through your nose, exhale out your mouth. Do this seven to 12 times or this as long as you like. How do you feel?

Notes:

_____

_____

_____

_____

_____

_____

_____

Surprises

Relax your resistance to the unexpected. Let your amazing journey unfold.

Notes:

_____

_____

_____

_____

_____

_____

_____

_____

_____

Give From Your Heart

What can you share with someone else that is important to you? Trust the right situation will present itself.

Notes:

_____

_____

_____

_____

_____

_____

_____

_____

_____

Thanking Circumstance

When confronted with negative circumstances, say "thank you." It is an opportunity to grow.

Notes:

_____

_____

_____

_____

_____

_____

_____

_____

_____

Ego Check

Situations happen in your life, to remind you of your ego. It takes practice to live with love and compassion.

Notes:

_____

_____

_____

_____

_____

_____

_____

_____

_____

Know When It Is Time to Go

Subtle signs are soft ways of letting you know changes are afoot. Your intuition is quick to recognize them, but your brain may try rationalizing. Recognize the fear talking, open your arms and welcome the change.

Notes:

_____

_____

_____

_____

_____

_____

_____

_____

Soaring

If you could soar across the sky, what bird would you be? Why?

Notes:

Loving Those That Hurt You

Most often the people you love and trust create the deepest wounds. Anger, regret and feeling like the victim puts salt on your wound. Nurturing your gash with self-love, surrounding yourself with positive distractions, will allow you to revisit the situation once you have healed. Loving the person for their wounds becomes easier.

Notes:

_____

_____

_____

_____

_____

_____

_____

Move Body Tension Away

You have a pattern of holding tension in a particular part of your body. Find a place you can be alone for a few minutes (it may be the bathroom). Take stock of you; where are you tense, your shoulder, neck, chest, hips? Place your hands on the area of tension; consciously push out and away from your body! You are changing the energy space around you, creating space for body relaxation.

Notes:

_____

_____

_____

_____

_____

_____

_____

Push Away Anger

Anger rises within you; you may notice this emotion after it has risen between your eyes. Using your hand, push the anger down and away from your body. Do it as often as you need to, to calm yourself. The other side of anger is hurt. Where are you hurt? Begin to heal that wound.

Notes:

_____

_____

_____

_____

_____

_____

_____

_____

Away With Depression

Depression and feeling like a victim may result from staying in your mind, over thinking the circumstances in your life. Bring the back of your hand between your eyes; push your hand up and away from your head. Push away the over thinking, depressing thoughts. Consciously ask for positive thoughts as you bring your palm toward your eyes. Do this as often as you need to.

Notes:

_____

_____

_____

_____

_____

_____

Sensitives

If you have a pattern of your mood changing for no reason, you may be picking up on someone else's energy.

Sensitive people feel and experience other peoples feelings. Go into the grounding stance, feet secure on the ground, stand or sit erect, using your hands push those feelings away from your stomach, chest and eyes. Breathe in warm, loving rays of the sun.

Notes:

_____

_____

_____

_____

_____

_____

_____

Invite Positive Thoughts

Feel both of your feet on the floor, you can be sitting or standing. Lying in bed works too. Invite sun rays filled with love and positive thoughts into your body. Use your arms and hands to gather the rays, send them to your body. Take a slow deep breath, imagine the sun warming you.

Notes:

_____

_____

_____

_____

_____

_____

_____

_____

The Victory Stance

There is no better feeling than feeling victorious! It is strong, and powerful connecting one to the rhythm of all life. Stand erect, your legs are as wide apart as is comfortable, feet evenly balanced, ribs are high, arms are up over your head in a V. Slowly turn your body from one side to the other, as if you were connecting with a crowd widely applauding your feat! Take a slow deep breath and smile, feel the energy of victory coming into your body. Do this whenever you are afraid, doubting yourself or need a boost. Invite success into your life. You can also do this sitting.

Notes:

_____

_____

_____

_____

_____

_____

Early Morning Messages

The early hours of the morning, between 3 and 5, can be opportunities to heal. Try to move past mind chatter and be with yourself; a message may come.

Notes:

_____

_____

_____

_____

_____

_____

_____

_____

_____

Like a Phoenix Rising

When your heart feels the most raw, miracles happen;
all of life can be felt in your being.

Notes:

Your Steps

Your daily life is full of steps taking you through your life. What kind of steps would you like to walk upon? Ornate steps, marble, wood, a dirt trail? Create the steps you would like to walk upon through your life.

Notes:

_____

_____

_____

_____

_____

_____

_____

_____

_____

Your Surroundings

You have created the steps you will use as you walk through your life at this moment in time. Create the environment around your steps, your self. What would you like to see?

Notes:

_____

_____

_____

_____

_____

_____

_____

_____

Never Doubt

Never doubt how amazing, wonderful and loved you are.

Notes:

_____

_____

_____

_____

_____

_____

_____

_____

_____

_____

Patience

Dragonflies wait years for their wings. Be patient, look at the beautiful spirits they are, know you are evolving perfectly.

Notes:

_____

_____

_____

_____

_____

_____

_____

_____

_____

_____

_____

About the Author

Francesca Fawn Russo was born on Long Island, New York, oldest child of Italian and Irish parents. She has lived and traveled across Europe, the United States, Costa Rica, and Brazil. The North Oregon Coast was her home for 30 years, until she moved to the high desert of Central Oregon in 2009.

Unknowingly experiencing sensitivity to the emotions of others, combined with family tragedy at an early age, created her desire to explore spirituality, both within herself and nature. It is here that Francesca has personally healed, and hopes her experiences will give others the tools they need to heal themselves.

Francesca has been a writer since childhood, a restaurant owner, a student of yoga, and a yoga therapist. She began training in the customs of indigenous spiritual healing in 1996. She is a licensed massage therapist, trained in cranial sacral and lymphatic therapy. Francesca combines her intuition, training as a spiritual practitioner, and yoga to personalize private sessions with people to help them empower their lives. She is available for private sessions, and can be contacted through her website, www.ufly4life.com.

Francesca's companion for the past nine years has been her German Shepherd, Yogi. She has one daughter who is married and lives in Oregon, where she teaches middle school.

Notes of Thanks

Giving, receiving, letting go, forgiving and opening my heart with love have and continue to be my journey. Cassie, my beautiful daughter, I love you. I wish you health, peace, love and joy on your journey through life.

I am most grateful for nature, the unconditional love and teachings I have and continue to receive amongst her diverse beauty has and will continue to shape my life.

To my mother, Nora Russo, and brother, Frank, thank you for the experiences we have shared together. For my sister, Judy, I wish you peace. To my father, in his absence, my journey of life began. I know he is proud.

To Nancy Burton, Kathleen Hickey, and Lena Lencek, your support and kindness have taught me how to receive. Shelly Hummel, your generous heart encompasses people and animals; thank you for opening your home to me when I had none.

To the men who have been in my life, thank you for being the instruments that taught me how to love myself.

My German Shepherd, Yogi, has been my main man. I am forever grateful for his love and protection.

To my friends and everyone I have met, you have all been an important part of my life – thank you.

To Lane MacManus, who introduced me to yoga and meditation, I'm forever grateful. To Valerie Pierce, Connie Flores, Zoe Willitts, owner of Shibui, and all the women I have worked with at Shibui while in Central Oregon, we are sisters. To my friend and editor, Helen Schmidling, thank you for your smile, your friendship and willingness to work with me.

Francesca

About You

Notes:

_____

_____

_____

_____

_____

_____

_____

_____

_____

_____

_____

Your Notes of Thanks

Notes:

_____

_____

_____

_____

_____

_____

_____

_____

_____

_____

Printed in the United States
By Bookmasters